PLAY LIKE A GIRL

TRACK AND FIELD

BY

EMILIE DUFRESNE

KidHaven
PUBLISHING

Published in 2020 by
KidHaven Publishing, an Imprint of Greenhaven Publishing, LLC
353 3rd Avenue
Suite 255
New York, NY 10010

Edited by: Madeline Tyler
Designed by: Danielle Jones

Cataloging-in-Publication Data

Names: Dufresne, Emilie.
Title: Track and field / Emilie Dufresne.
Description: New York : KidHaven Publishing, 2020. | Series: Play like a girl | Includes glossary and index.
Identifiers: ISBN 9781534530997 (pbk.) | ISBN 9781534530089 (library bound) | ISBN 9781534531314 (6 pack) | ISBN 9781534530935 (ebook)
Subjects: LCSH: Track and field--Juvenile literature.
Classification: LCC GV1060.55 D847 2020 | DDC 796.42--dc23

Printed in the United States of America

CPSIA compliance information: Batch #BS19KL: For further information contact Greenhaven Publishing LLC, New York, New York at 1-844-317-7404.

Please visit our website, www.greenhavenpublishing.com.
For a free color catalog of all our high-quality books, call toll free 1-844-317-7404 or fax 1-844-317-7405.

IMAGE CREDITS

Cover - Stephen Rees, marpan, cocoo, Inked Pixels, wavebreakmedia. 3 - marpan. 4 -Denis Kuvaev, Romariolen, Inked Pixels. 5 - dotshock, Denis Kuvaev. 6 - Alfaguarilla. 7 - Natursports, WoodysPhotos. 8&9 - Pete Saloutos. 10 - Diego Barbieri, Herbert Kratky, CP DC Press. 11 - EvrenKalinbacak, Hafiz Johari, Shahjehan. 12 - StockphotoVideo, Aspen Photo, EvrenKalinbacak. 13 - Aleksandar Kamasi, EvrenKalinbacak. 14 - Jacob Lund, MinDof. 15 - Dean Drobot, mezzotint, a katz. 16 - Stefan Schurr, CHRISTIANTO, Natursports. 17 - sirtravelalot, John Kasawa, wavebreakmedia, JM-Design. 18-19 -Marius Antonescu. 20 - Andrey Burmakin, CP DC Press. 21 - sportpoint, muzsy. 22 - LifetimeStock, Alfaguarilla. 23 - Denis Kuvaev, CP DC Press. 24 -Alfaguarilla, Athletics Federation of India [CC BY-SA 4.0 (https://creativecommons.org/licenses/by-sa/4.0)], via Wikimedia Commons. 25 - ian_fromblighty [CC BY 2.0 (https://creativecommons.org/licenses/by/2.0)], via Wikimedia Commons, Doha Stadium Plus Qatar from Doha, Qatar [CC BY 2.0 (https://creativecommons.org/licenses/by/2.0)], via Wikimedia Commons. 26 - Mascha Tace, Africa Studio. 27 - Vera Larina. 28 - Bundesarchiv, Bild 183-1990-0819-002 / CC-BY-SA 3.0 [CC BY-SA 3.0 de (https://creativecommons.org/licenses/by-sa/3.0/de/deed.en)], Alfaguarilla, wavebreakmedia. 29 - Erik van Leeuwen [GFDL (http://www.gnu.org/copyleft/fdl.html) or GFDL (http://www.gnu.org/copyleft/fdl.html)], Palyvoda2006 [CC0], via Wikimedia Commons, "Courtesy Ronald Reagan Library. [Public domain], via Wikimedia Commons, Africa Studio. 30 - Mark Herreid, sirtravelalot. Illustrations by Danielle Jones. Images are courtesy of Shutterstock.com. With thanks to Getty Images, Thinkstock Photo and iStockphoto.

CONTENTS

Words that look like <u>this</u> are track and field lingo. Learn more about them on page 8.

Words that look like **THIS** are explained in the glossary on page 31.

THE BASICS

PEP TALK

So, you want to take part in track and field? This book will teach you all about what to say, what to wear, and what to do. From learning the lingo to earning a place in the Hall of Fame, this book will give you the know-how!

GRAB YOUR FRIENDS AND SNEAKERS – IT'S TIME TO PRACTICE!

Track and field is the name for lots of different events. These events can be put into three main categories: running, jumping, and throwing.

DIFFERENT PEOPLE HAVE DIFFERENT STRENGTHS AND ARE BETTER AT DIFFERENT EVENTS.

Some track and field events are very quick, such as the 100-meter sprint; these events take a lot of strength and speed. Other events are more about ENDURANCE. All athletes have to train really hard for their specific event, so that they can perform to the best of their ability.

Most track and field events are individual. This means that instead of playing on a team, one person competes against other individuals. Some events, such as relays, involve athletes competing together on teams, usually for their country or region. These athletes have to work together to win.

THE TYPES

INDOOR AND OUTDOOR

As the names suggest, indoor track and field events are held inside an arena, while outdoor track and field events are held outside. Running events include sprints, hurdles, steeplechases, and relays. Jumping events include the pole vault, high jump, long jump, and triple jump. Throwing events include the discus throw, hammer throw, shot put, and javelin throw.

A very **PRESTIGIOUS** event is the heptathlon. This is an event that combines seven track and field events and takes place over two days. On the first day, the athletes compete in the 100-meter hurdles, the high jump, the shot put throw, and the 200-meter sprint. On the second day, the athletes compete in the long jump, the javelin throw, and the 800-meter race.

HEPTATHLETE NAFISSATOU THIAM AT THE 2018 EUROPEAN CHAMPIONSHIPS

ATHLETES HAVE TO BE ABLE TO DO WELL IN ALL OF THESE EVENTS TO WIN A HEPTATHLON.

RACE WALKING

Race walking is where athletes have to cover a set distance, usually 20 kilometers (12.4 miles) or 50 kilometers (31 miles) as fast as they can, while always having at least one foot on the ground. This event commonly takes place outside on the streets.

RACE WALKING EVENT

THIS SPORT MAY NOT LOOK DIFFICULT, BUT IT IS VERY PHYSICALLY DEMANDING!

CROSS-COUNTRY RUNNING

Cross-country races are mostly run in either grassy or woodland areas, but might also occur along gravel paths, roads, and steep hills. The athletes have to battle with natural **OBSTACLES** while using their strength and endurance.

THERE ARE ALSO PARALYMPIC ATHLETIC EVENTS FOR PEOPLE WITH ALL DIFFERENT TYPES OF DISABILITIES.

THE LINGO

The lingo, the slang, the vocab. Whatever you call it, learning the words behind specific sports can be a very daunting task! Here are some of the terms and weirder words that will help you talk the track and field talk in no time.

FAULTS

When an athlete does something they are not supposed to, such as running over the fault line in the long and triple jump.

ARENA

The large building in which many athletic events take place. There is often seating around the outside of the track and field so that people can watch the events.

FALSE START

When an athlete moves before the starting gun has gone off, giving them an unfair advantage. The race is restarted when this happens.

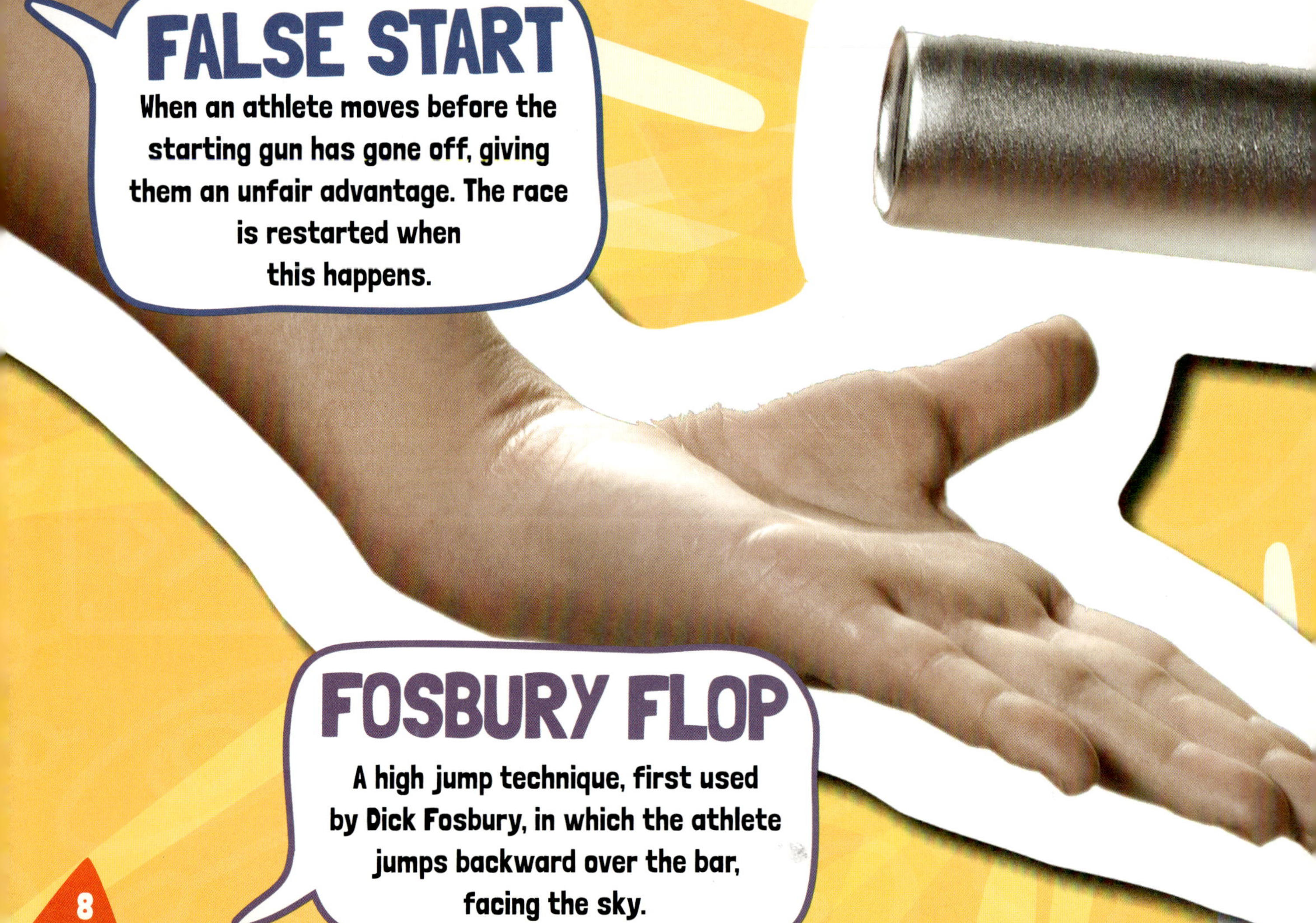

FOSBURY FLOP

A high jump technique, first used by Dick Fosbury, in which the athlete jumps backward over the bar, facing the sky.

HURDLES

Light fences or gates that can be moved. Athletes try to jump over these, but if they fail, the hurdle will easily fall over, letting them pass. However, it will slow the athlete down.

STARTING BLOCKS

The equipment used by sprinters to begin a race. Athletes place their feet in these to get the best possible start to a race.

STAGGERED STARTS

When athletes begin at different points on a curved racetrack so that they all run the same distance.

RELAYS

An event in which four athletes join together to make one team. Each member of a team takes a turn to run a set distance with a baton. As they finish their part of the race, they pass the baton on to the next runner on their team, and so on.

SPRINT

To run as fast as you can for a set distance using all your power and strength.

THE TRACK AND FIELD EVENTS

100-METER, 200-METER, AND 400-METER SPRINTS

Athletes begin at the starting blocks and then run at full speed for the set distance in the quickest time possible.

HURDLES AND STEEPLECHASE

Hurdles are similar to the sprinting events, except athletes must also jump over a certain number of hurdles placed at equal intervals along the run. The steeplechase is where athletes run a course that has fixed barriers and water jumps that the athletes have to contend with.

MIDDLE- AND LONG-DISTANCE RUNS

After sprints come middle- and long-distance runs. These are longer than the sprinting events and therefore require strategy and endurance. The athletes must think about how they are going to pace themselves and where to put in the most effort during the race.

HAVING A RUNNING STRATEGY IS WHEN AN ATHLETE HAS MADE PLANS FOR HOW THEY ARE GOING TO RUN A RACE BEFORE IT STARTS.

SHOT PUT

Shot put is a "putting" event. Putting a ball, rather than throwing it, means pushing it away from you using your strength. The shot is a heavy metal ball which the athletes must put as far away from the circle they stand in as possible. Athletes hold the shot close to the neck, then glide or spin around, gaining **MOMENTUM** before releasing the ball.

HAMMER THROW

Athletes must throw a metal ball as far as they can. The ball is attached to a handle by a steel wire. Similar to the shot put, athletes make three to four spins to build up momentum before releasing the hammer.

DISCUS THROW

The discus is a heavy metal disc. Athletes must throw the disc as far as possible. Unlike the hammer throw and shot put, athletes are only allowed to spin one and a half times to build momentum.

JAVELIN THROW

For the javelin throw, an athlete must throw a spear-shaped stick as far as possible. The athletes can run toward the foul line to build momentum and then must throw the javelin as far as they can.

POLE VAULT

The pole vault is a jumping event in which athletes use a pole to push themselves high into the air and then push themselves over a horizontal pole without knocking it off. The athletes do a long run-up, push the pole into the ground, and use **KINETIC ENERGY** to get them as high into the air as possible.

HIGH JUMP

The high jump is similar to the pole vault, except that the athletes can only use their bodies and the momentum they build up during their run to clear the horizontal pole. Most athletes use a technique called the <u>Fosbury Flop</u>.

LONG JUMP

For the long jump, an athlete runs as fast as they can up to a board and then leaps as far as they can off of it. They push their bodies as far as possible and then land in the sandpit. The athlete who jumps the farthest distance wins.

TRIPLE JUMP

The triple jump is similar to the long jump except that, after running a short way, the athletes must then perform a hop and a step before jumping as far as they can into the sandpit.

THE UNIFORM

Most athletes wear tight-fitting tops and shorts. This makes them have less AIR RESISTANCE, meaning there will be less to stop them from performing at their best. These types of clothing can also help prevent accidental faults in events such as the pole vault and high jump. This is because baggy clothes may touch or get caught on the poles.

Sprinters also need specially ADAPTED shoes that have spikes on their soles. These spikes grip into the track as the athlete is running. This stops them from sliding or skidding. It also means that all the force they put into their run goes into pushing them forward.

PARALYMPICS

Lots of paralympic athletes have highly advanced and **SPECIALIZED** gear. One example is the running blade. The running blade is used for athletes who are missing part of one or both legs. The blades are often made of very light **CARBON FIBER**. They are specially designed to store kinetic energy, a bit like a spring.

BLADES CAN BE USED FOR MANY DIFFERENT TRACK AND FIELD EVENTS, INCLUDING MOST RUNNING EVENTS.

Some athletes use a wheelchair to compete in road and track races. Those who compete in these sports need their wheelchairs to be streamlined, lightweight, and stable so that they can perform to the best of their ability. The wheelchairs have to be specially adapted for racing.

DIFFERENT SPORTS NEED DIFFERENT TYPES OF WHEELCHAIRS THAT ARE ESPECIALLY FOR THAT SPORT.

THE EQUIPMENT

All the different track and field events need specific equipment. Here is some of the most important.

For many sprinters, the starting blocks are an essential piece of equipment. The athletes can adjust the starting blocks to make sure they get the best start to a race. They give runners something to push against and get their muscles ready for action.

The high jump and pole vault both require landing mats so that the athletes can land their jumps safely. These mats need to be in the right place and be deep enough to stop an athlete from hurting themselves.

Lots of the objects used in the throwing events are standardized. Standardized objects make the sport fair by making sure every throw is taken with the same type of equipment.

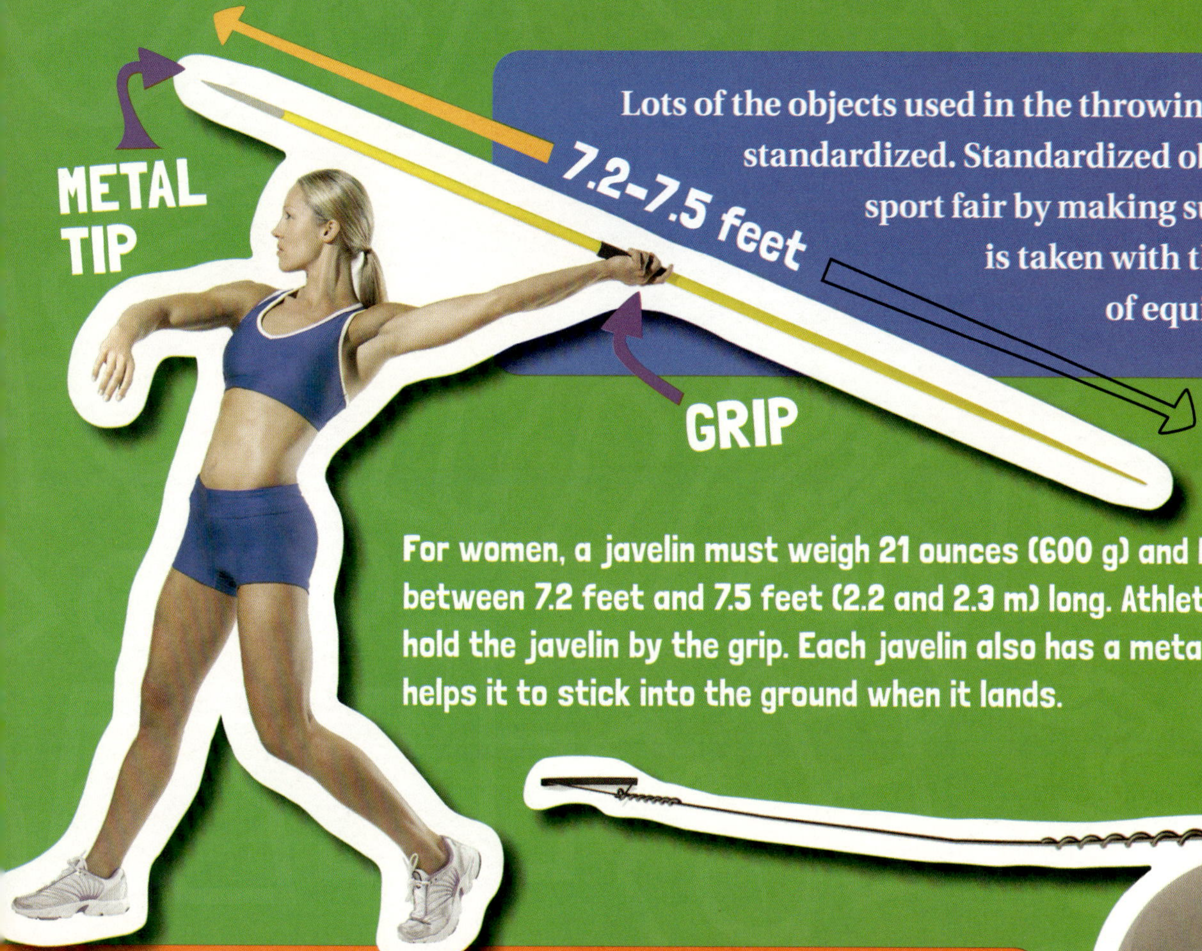

For women, a javelin must weigh 21 ounces (600 g) and be between 7.2 feet and 7.5 feet (2.2 and 2.3 m) long. Athletes must hold the javelin by the grip. Each javelin also has a metal tip that helps it to stick into the ground when it lands.

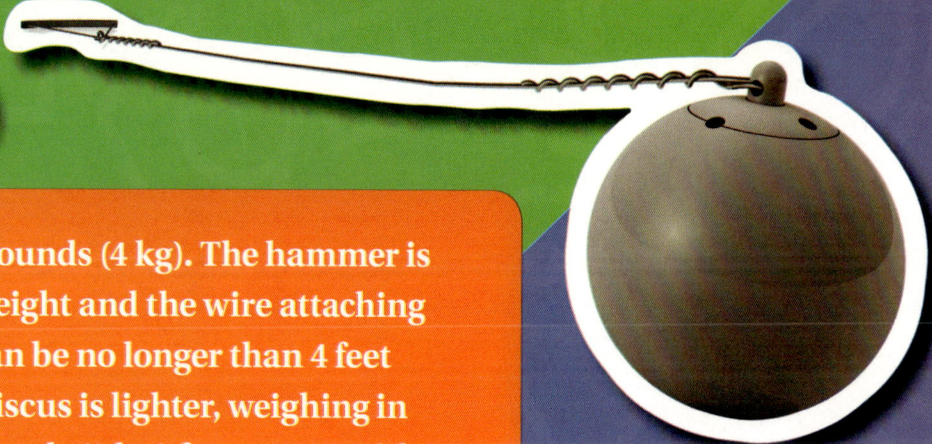

Women's shots weigh 8.8 pounds (4 kg). The hammer is also 8.8 pounds (4 kg) in weight and the wire attaching it to the handle can be no longer than 4 feet (1.22 m). The discus is lighter, weighing in at only 2.2 pounds (1 kg) for women with a diameter of 7.1 inches (18 cm).

THE TRACK AND FIELD

Lots of events take place on the track and field, which will look something like this. The throwing and jumping events happen on a field inside the running track.

One lap around the entire track is about 400 meters.

Each lane around the track has a slightly different length. The lane on the outside will be longer than the lane on the inside. To make sure each runner travels the same distance, most races use staggered starts.

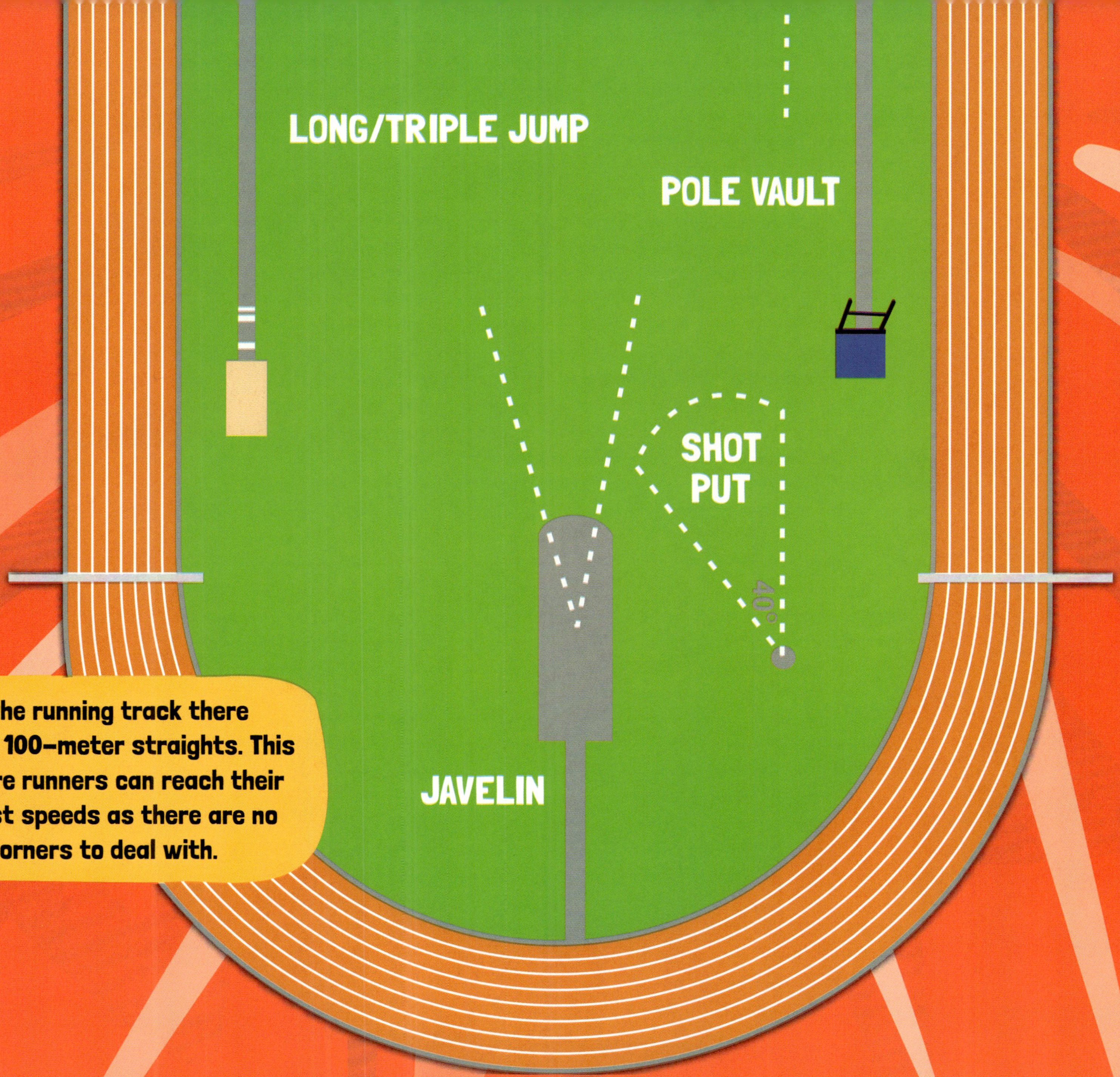

On the running track there are two 100-meter straights. This is where runners can reach their fastest speeds as there are no corners to deal with.

THE RULES

As all the events are so different, each individual event has its own set of rules. There are basic rules that can be grouped into running rules, jumping rules, and throwing rules.

RUNNING RULES

- Athletes running distances up to 400 meters should stay in their lane for the whole race
- Athletes running distances longer than 400 meters should begin in their lane but can then move into other lanes. However, they should not contact other runners when doing so.
- Athletes should begin every race with their whole body behind the start line
- Athletes should not commit a false start, also known as "jumping the gun"
- Athletes who commit a false start are disqualified from the event
- Athletes must not block, stop, or shove another athlete in order to stop them from gaining an advantage

JUMPING RULES

- The runway for all jumps must be 131 feet (40 m) long
- Triple jumpers must use the same leg to take off and land the hop
- Long and triple jumpers must not take off past the foul line
- Somersaults are not permitted in the long and triple jump
- Long and triple jumpers must land in the sandpit
- The mark in the sand closest to the jump line is measured
- If pole vaulters and high jumpers knock the pole off, it counts as a foul

THROWING RULES

- Athletes must stay within the throwing circle for the discus, shot put, and hammer throw
- They can touch the board around the circle but not place their foot on top of it
- Only in the javelin throw can athletes take a run-up
- The object that is thrown or putted must always land within a marked area that is different in each sport

THE EVENTS

RECREATIONAL AND REGIONAL TEAMS

If you do track and field at school, or practice **RECREATIONALLY**, and you want to start competing, there are lots of ways you can get involved. Ask a teacher, parent, or sports coach how to become part of a local training team or competition.

RECREATIONAL TRACK AND FIELD PRACTICE

THE BIG LEAGUES

As athletes get better and better, they can start competing at higher levels. After regional events or competitions come national ones. This means you compete against athletes from all over your country. Then comes competing internationally, which means representing your country. There are lots of championships and games for different **CONTINENTS** around the world, including Africa, Asia, Europe, and the Americas.

EUROPEAN ATHLETICS CHAMPIONSHIP, 2018

WORLD TOURNAMENTS

There are many international track and field competitions in which countries from around the world compete. Some of these include the **COMMONWEALTH** Games, **IAAF** Continental Cup, and the World Championships.

IAAF WORLD CHAMPIONSHIPS

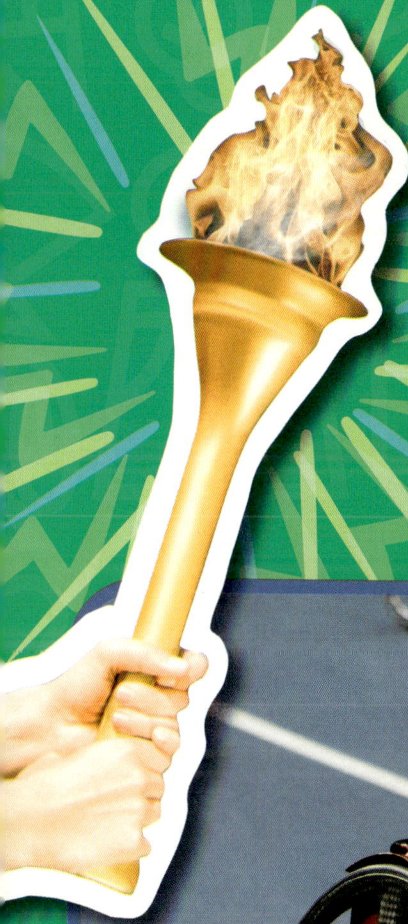

THE OLYMPICS

One of the most prestigious world tournaments is the Olympics. Lots of countries compete in a variety of games, including many track and field events. Track and field is in both the Olympic Games and the Paralympic Games.

100-METER SPRINT FINAL, 2016 PARALYMPIC GAMES

THE ONES TO WATCH

There are some very talented female athletes to look out for. Let's find out some more about them.

DINA ASHER-SMITH

FACT FILE:

Date of Birth:
December 4, 1995

Country of Birth:
United Kingdom

Events:
100 meter, 200 meter, 100-meter relay

Asher-Smith already has eight gold medals to her name, and she's still very young! The world can't wait to see where she'll go.

SWAPNA BARMAN

FACT FILE:

Date of Birth:
October 29, 1996

Country of Birth:
India

Event:
Heptathlon

Making a stir in the Asian Games and the Asian Championships with two golds, Barman is definitely a heptathlon hero. In the 2018 Asian Games, she competed even though she had a terrible jaw ache. She went on to collapse in the final event, the 800 meter, but already had enough points to claim a victory. What a trooper!

PLAY LIKE A GIRL

HANNAH COCKROFT

FACT FILE:

Date of Birth:
July 30, 1992

Country of Birth:
United Kingdom

Event:
Wheelchair racing

Cockroft is also known as "Hurricane Hannah," which isn't surprising considering that she currently holds the world records for the 100-meter, 200-meter, 400-meter, 800-meter, and 1500-meter wheelchair races. In 2013, Cockroft was awarded an **MBE** for her services to athletics.

SANDRA PERKOVIĆ

FACT FILE:

Date of Birth:
June 21, 1990

Country of Birth:
Croatia

Event:
Discus throw

Perković is a devilish discus thrower. She has won two Olympic golds and has even won gold at five European Championships in a row. The first of these was won at the 2010 Championships, where she became the youngest-ever woman to win gold at the competition.

THE HALL

There is a great history of female athletes. Let's take a look at some of the best of the best.

Fanny Blankers-Koen, a Dutch track and field athlete, proved everyone wrong when at the age of 30, and being a mother of two, she won four gold medals at the 1948 Olympics. This earned her the nickname "The Flying Housewife," proving that moms are even tougher than we already thought! She was awarded "Female Athlete of the Century" in 1999 by the IAAF.

Competing as a heptathlete, Dame Jessica Ennis-Hill is a three-time world champion, Olympic gold medalist, and has eight gold medals overall. But this isn't where her achievements end. In 2017, after she had retired, Ennis-Hill was awarded a **DBE** for her services to athletics.

OF FAME

Wilma Rudolph was the first American woman to win three Olympic gold medals in a single Olympic Games. She enjoyed great fame in the 1960s and used this fame to promote track and field, but also to fight for **CIVIL RIGHTS** and **WOMEN'S RIGHTS**. She became a role model for black female athletes across the world.

Irena Szewińska was a Polish sprinter who mastered multiple events. She is the only athlete in history to have held the world record for the 100-meter, the 200-meter, and the 400-meter race at the same time. Plus, in 1974, Szewińska became the first woman to run the 400-meter race in under 50 seconds.

THE FACTS AND STATS

HEIKE DRECHSLER IS A LONG JUMPER WHO CURRENTLY HOLDS THE WOMEN'S INDOOR WORLD RECORD OF 24.2 FEET (7.37 M), WHICH SHE SET IN 1988. HER DISTANCE STILL HASN'T BEEN BEATEN TO THIS DAY.

THE MEN'S HAMMER THROW BECAME AN OLYMPIC SPORT IN 1900, BUT IT WAS 100 YEARS LATER THAT THE WOMEN'S HAMMER THROW FINALLY BECAME AN OLYMPIC SPORT.

THE POLES IN THE POLE VAULT USED TO BE MADE OF WOOD BUT ARE NOW MADE OF FIBERGLASS TO PREVENT THEM FROM SNAPPING.

ONE OF THE MOST SUCCESSFUL FEMALE TRACK AND FIELD ATHLETES IN OLYMPIC HISTORY IS MERLENE OTTEY. SHE IS A JAMAICAN FORMER SPRINTER WHO, BETWEEN THE 1980 AND THE 2000 OLYMPIC GAMES, WON 9 MEDALS: THREE SILVER AND SIX BRONZE.

THE RECORD FOR THE LONGEST FEMALE TRIPLE JUMP IS HELD BY INESSA KRAVETS, WHO JUMPED AN IMPRESSIVE 50.85 FEET (15.5 M) IN 1995. HER RECORD REMAINS UNBEATEN TO THIS DAY.

FLORENCE GRIFFITH-JOYNER CURRENTLY HOLDS THE WOMEN'S WORLD RECORD FOR THE FASTEST 100-METER RUN, WITH A TIME OF JUST 10.49 SECONDS! SHE HAS HELD THIS RECORD SINCE 1988.

YOUR TRAINING

If any of the track and field events sound like the thing for you, why not start practicing or training? Ask all your friends if they want to give it a go. If you have a gym with a track or an outdoor track and field at your school, why not give it a try?

There are so many track and field events to try, you are sure to enjoy at least one! You never know – if you enjoy it, and you keep practicing, you might be in the Hall of Fame one day!

GLOSSARY

adapted	to be changed for a specific use
air resistance	a force that pushes back against an object moving through the air
carbon fiber	a very strong, but very lightweight, material
civil rights	the rights a person should have to be free and treated equally
Commonwealth	a group of countries, including the UK, Canada, and Australia, that used to be part of the British Empire
continents	very large areas of land that are commonly made up of many countries, such as Africa and Europe
DBE	Dame of the British Empire, an award given for outstanding achievements on a national level in the UK, often for inspirational and committed work
endurance	being able to do something that is mentally or physically tiring for a long time
IAAF	International Association of Athletics Federations; the governing body for the sport of track and field across the world
kinetic energy	a type of energy that refers to movement
MBE	Member of the British Empire, an award given for an outstanding achievement or service to the community
momentum	the power and speed of a moving object
obstacles	things that get in the way of something or someone
prestigious	having an important and highly regarded status
recreationally	to do something for fun rather than professionally
specialized	made to have a specific purpose or use
women's rights	rights for women that men already have

INDEX